Gavin Ewart was born in 1916. He has worked in advertising and for the British Council. He is now a freelance writer. His books of verse include *Poems and Songs* (1939), *Londoners* (1964), *Pleasures of the Flesh* (1966), *The Deceptive Grin of the Gravel Porters* (1968) and *The Gavin Ewart Show* (1971).

Zulfikar Ghose was born in Pakistan in 1935 and emigrated to England in 1952. He went to Keele University and then worked as a cricket and hockey correspondent of the *Observer* for five years. Since 1969 he has been living in the U.S.A. He has published three books of poems, *The Loss of India* (1964), *Jets of Orange* (1967) and *The Violent West* (1972).

Brian Stanley Johnson was born in 1933, educated at King's College, London, published his first novel, *Travelling People,* in 1963, and his first collection of poetry a year later. His third novel, *Trawl,* won the Somerset Maugham Award for 1967 and his film, *You're Human Like the Rest of Them,* won the Grand Prix at both the Tours and Melbourne festivals in 1968. He edited two anthologies, *The Evacuees* and *All Bull – the National Serviceman.* His last book was *Christy Malry's Own Double Entry.* Brian Johnson died in 1973.

Penguin Modern Poets

25

GAVIN EWART
ZULFIKAR GHOSE
B. S. JOHNSON

Penguin Books

Penguin Books Ltd, Harmondsworth, Middlesex, England
Penguin Books Inc., 7110 Ambassador Road, Baltimore, Maryland 21207, U.S.A.
Penguin Books Australia Ltd, Ringwood, Victoria, Australia
Penguin Books Canada Ltd, 41 Steelcase Road West, Markham, Ontario, Canada
Penguin Books (N.Z.) Ltd, 182–190 Wairau Road, Auckland 10, New Zealand

—

First published 1975

—

Copyright © Penguin Books Ltd, 1975

—

Made and printed in Great Britain by
Cox & Wyman Ltd, London, Reading and Fakenham
Set in Monotype Garamond

Contents

CONTENTS

CONTENTS

CONTENTS

Acknowledgements

The poems by Gavin Ewart are taken from *Poems and Songs,* The Fortune Press, 1939 (now out of print), *Pleasures of the Flesh,* Alan Ross, 1966, *The Deceptive Grin of the Gravel Porters,* London Magazine Editions, 1968, and *The Gavin Ewart Show,* Trigram Press, 1971.

The poems by Zulfikar Ghose are taken from *The Loss of India,* Routledge & Kegan Paul, 1964 (now out of print), *Jets of Orange,* Macmillan, 1967, and *The Violent West,* Macmillan, 1972.

The poems by B. S. Johnson are taken from *Poems,* Constable, 1964, and *Poems Two,* Trigram Press, 1972.

GAVIN EWART

Miss Twye

Miss Twye was soaping her breasts in her bath
When she heard behind her a meaning laugh
And to her amazement she discovered
A wicked man in the bathroom cupboard.

Audenesque for an Initiation

Don't forget the things we taught you by the broken water-wheel,
Don't forget the middle classes fight much harder going downhill,

Don't forget that new proscriptions are being posted now and then,
Dr Johnson, Dr Leavis and the other Grand Old Men –

Although they've very often told us that they try to do their best,
Are they up to the Full Fruit Standard, would they pass the Spelling
Test?

– Because we've got our eyes to keyholes, we know everything they've
done,
Lecturing on minor poets. 'Literature is quite good fun.'

And if you should try to fool us, imitate them, do the same,
We'll refuse your dummy bullets, we've had time to take our aim.

We've been drinking stagnant water for some twenty years or more
While the politicians slowly planned a bigger reservoir.

But we've dammed a different river, the water-wheel is going again.
Now we've stopped designing sweaters and we've started in to train.

We've given up the Georgian poets, teaching dance bands how to croon,
Bicycling in coloured goggles underneath a pallid moon.

We've destroyed the rotting signposts, made holes in all the pleasure
boats;
We'll pull down ancestral castles when we've time to swim the moats.

When we've practised we shall beat you with our Third or Fourth
Fifteen,
In spite of Royalists on the touchline. 'Oh, well played, Sir!' 'Keep it
clean!'

Our backs are fast as motor-cycles, all our forwards 20-stone.
Each of them can score unaided, running strongly on his own.

Every minute scouts give signals, come reporting what they've seen.
'Captain Ferguson is putting.' 'Undermine the 18th green.'

Before next month we'll storm the clubhouse. Messages are coming
    through:
'Darwin, doing crossword puzzles, tries to find the missing clue.'

The *Times* Third Leaders are decoded, pigeon-holed for future use;
Tennyson has been convicted of incessant self-abuse.

We've been sending notes to Priestley, orange pips to J. C. Squire –
'Don't defend the trench you're holding.' 'Now the fat is in the fire.'

We've got control of all the railways and the perfume factories,
We're supercharged and have connection with the strongest batteries.

So if you feel like playing truant, remember that the game is up
Or you'll find that quite politely you've been sold a nasty pup.

Public School

A surname in this place
Is fitting. Keeps reserved
Emotional platoons
Positioned in the eyes,
Attentive for a word.

The pupils here obey
The friend's didactic voice,
Are wakeful at a smile,
Can answer questions, lie,
Express polite surprise.

If one should raise a hand,
Ask question out of turn,
Then discipline would die,
Order be broken and
The other's eye be stern.

Wanting Out

They're putting Man-Fix on my hair. And through the window
Comes a naked woman with a big whatnot. Oops! I'm away
To a country where the fantasies can be controlled.
Modestly I want to live, modestly. Where the Herr Baron
Takes an Eiswein from the cellar, cradles it gently
In the tiny frozen hands of an echt Deutsch Mimi.
Where the quiet roebuck surround the hunting lodge,
Where the peasants, if they wanted, could shave with their hats.

Take me down to a Lustschloss in the year 1900,
Give me tea on the lawn of a vicarage garden,
Put me in a punt with all my little girl friends,
Let the dreams grow into the leafy sexbooks.
I want a magnifying glass and a knowledge of Coptic
And a box in the British Museum for the last performance of
Hamlet.

Barbary

I pace the Fourth Floor like a quarter deck,
My windows square portholes on the sailing traffic,
My executive suite littered with charts.
From raids on the surrounding country
I bring back the new business
Sailing close, close to the wind.

I am surrounded by captured beauties,
The sexy secretaries come mincing in,
In it for the money.
And this is also the Good Ship Venus
Where fantasies are playing in the rigging
Like St Elmo's Fire.

I shall have a memo sent to all the staff
Prohibiting collections for those who leave
To go to other agencies.
I shall bank a good many thousands
This year. I shall stop my ears
When they fire an old copywriter from a cannon.
After all, I am an alert, brisk trader –
And everyone can recognize the Jolly Roger.

A Secular Saint?

Tell
How his father taught him to shoot
Rabbits straight from the shoulder.
How he went on the great Educational Pilgrimage,
Suffered under Caesar and Cicero
And was unjustly beaten.
How he underwent the terrifying boredom of war,
The tantalizing sorrows of impotence
When every girl was a mantrap.
Tell
Of the five years' analysis in the wilderness,
The marriage and the two children,
The crowded flats in unfashionable districts,
The continual spreading of The Word,
The three books of poetry in the British Museum.
Tell
How he was sacked in the takeover city,
How he discovered Italy and a foolproof method
Of killing time in North London,
How his goodness was never recognized,
How he died and was translated.
Tell.

A Christmas Message

In the few warm weeks
   before Christmas and the cold
the Toy Department is organized like a factory floor.
They're using epitaxial planar techniques
   in the labs. The toys are sold
and there's rationalized packaging and at the hot core

of the moving mass
   sweats a frost-powdered Father Christmas
in a red dressing-gown and an off-white beard.
What he wants most is a draught Bass.
   On a dry Hellenic isthmus
Zeus was a god who was equally hated and feared;

England is a Peloponnese
   and Father Christmas a poor old sod
like any other, autochthonous. Who believes
in the beard and the benevolence? Even in Greece
   or Rome there is only a bogus God
for children under five. Those he loves, he deceives.

GAVIN EWART

Warm to the Cuddly-Toy Charm
of a Koala Bear

It's dull in the huge palace where I live.
The basement's stuffed with seduced handkerchiefs.
A global war would do, or a new revolution,
To dissipate the gloom of early spring.
Everything's wet – but most the men and women –
Outside, where the long rains drip from the trees.

I'm lonely. There's nobody here but me.
The vintages go round and round in my head
A merry-go-round I suppose I ought to call it.
Cobwebbed bottles and a thousand dirty glasses,
One in my hand.

Enthusiasm belongs *outside* – and mostly it's bogus.
I live in a mood, with a boozer's conk,
I'm no Prince Charming,
But I'm genuine, genuine, true to my dirty self.

Secrets of the Alcove

Quand' ero paggio . . .
I must have been adorable (I was certainly stupid).
The then Provost of King's
Chased me down two flights of stairs at a party.
Nearly twenty years later
A girl ran a hundred yards down a platform in Paris
In high-heeled shoes to kiss me.

All answered with a coldish heart.

Who has not had their little successes?
Inner absorption breaks into a rash of pride,
Shows in the visible signs of bad behaviour.
I regret my calmness in the face of love,
It bothers me like an unopened letter
Returned to sender, that now will never be read.

A Warning

A little fat genius is sitting there,
Small head, big belly.
A lot of brains under a little hair,
His sex organs – smelly.

That's the way it is with a genius,
He's always a bit odd.
He may have girl friends, grow zinnias,
But he thinks he's a god.

Don't expect ordinary behaviour,
Or a guide to morals.
A genius is never a Saviour –
He only looks to his laurels.

The Dildo

(One of Eight Awful Animals)

The Dildo is a big heavy cumbersome sort of bird,
Supposed extinct for many years but its voice is often heard
Booming and blasting over the marshes and moors
With the harsh note of Lesbos and the great outdoors.
The Dildo wears tweed skirts and Twenties elastic-thighed
    knickers
And smokes black cheroots and still calls films 'the flickers'.
It wears pork-pie hats and is really one of the boys,
It has initiated many pretty girls into forbidden joys.

It has an eye-glass in one eye, and its bad-taste jokes are myriad,
Such as the one about Emily Brontë's Last Period,
And a good many others that are best left unsaid,
Buried in the old laughter, as the dead bury the dead.

The Dildo is quite frankly worshipped by some members of the
    community,
Who consider that even its name cannot be taken in vain with
    impunity
As it hops heavily about on its one wooden leg –
But most real Nature-lovers think it should be taken down
    a peg.

Office Friendships

Eve is madly in love with Hugh
And Hugh is keen on Jim.
Charles is in love with very few
And few are in love with him.

Myra sits typing notes of love
With romantic pianist's fingers.
Dick turns his eyes to the heavens above
Where Fran's divine perfume lingers.

Nicky is rolling eyes and tits
And flaunting her wiggly walk.
Everybody is thrilled to bits
By Clive's suggestive talk.

Sex suppressed will go berserk,
But it keeps us all alive.
It's a wonderful change from wives and work
And it ends at half past five.

Pi-Dog and Wish-Cat

When Pi-Dog and Wish-Cat sat down for a meal,
His and Hers on their bowls, there was a great deal
For them both to pronounce on, deny and discuss.
Their words were all taped and have come down to us.

Pi-Dog said he believed in a Man In The Sky
Who would end the whole world in a flaming great fry
Most delicious for dogs (who of course would be spared),
And the bones of their enemies equally shared.

Wish-Cat said, purring, how Love was the thing
And was easily captured by using a ring;
How Love would in rapture squeak louder than mice
And live happy as dreams. And wasn't it nice?

When the meal was all over they both wanted more –
And Pi-Dog dragged Wish-Cat down onto the floor.
Pi-Dog bit hard and deep, and she clawed at his eyes.
Now they both of them sleep where it says HERE LIES.

Diary of a Critic

Had two poets for lunch. This afternoon
Got my teeth into a fat biography.
Went down quite well. I always try
To taste the pages, savour line by line,
Remember what Richards on a Cambridge blackboard
Slyly wrote out in his peculiar spelling.

Reviewing dulls the palate.

'Placed' a few contemporary writers.
Took Auden down a peg, moved up Lowell,
Established a new End of Term Order,
Prizes to Eliot Major, Betjeman Minor.
Several new scholarship boys are coming on.
Must be ready. Never be left behind,
A fuddy-duddy wound in a black gown.

Beyond the pleasure principle. No more enjoy.
Never get plastered on the fine new wine.
Mem. The Meaning of Meaning. Stand firm.

Venus in Furs

There's a new opera called *I Masochisti*
With words by Freud and music by Bellini.
The first night's full of scented, furry women,
You can't have them. The conductor's baton
Puts an embargo on all base desires.
Under gold lamé the big nipples swell
In crescendo. You're the muted horn
That sings of knighthood in the foyer bar.

Bullish, a stalled industrialist. He has it made.
His big bass voice comes straight up from his balls.
Whipped by desires, you're the derided one.
Nobody wants you, loves you, likes you.
Such marvellous deprivation! Can it last?

Beginnings

In the vast antheap of the world
one little ant thinks differently.

In the snarled traffic of metropolis
a small family car crashes the lights.

Under a tailored and conventional suit
a heart beats out a naked rhythm.

Like a roomsize coloured balloon
a man blows up a religion till it bursts.

Somebody somewhere begins to unpick the stitches
in the bright battle flag of glory.

Daddyo

My hearing deadens. My eyes
aren't good in artificial light.
The memory wobbles. But
that's enough of that.

So clearly I remember
what a harsh crass old man
my father seemed
thirty years ago.

But he was the bright boy
from Edinburgh, the medico who won
hundreds of pounds of weighty scholarships.
A big attacking surgeon.

My mind shrank under the barking knife.

Now it's my turn
to be the red-faced fool
that sons hate, tittered at
by sneering miniskirts.

It's strange to wear
a dead man's shoes, to know
exactly where
each one pinches.

The Deceptive Grin of the Gravel Porters

Through the rain forests, up a long river,
over greensand and clay and red earth,
they toil like ants in their long procession,
hacking at difficulties that grow and close again,
covering once more the path behind them.

Following these unimportant carriers of the unimportant,
we seldom see them. When we do, they grin.
After the bad patches they turn with a kind of smirk
and beckon us. There are large animals too
that rustle through the hemispheres.

Travelling over chalk to a familiar sea
is all we dream of where the trees are strangled
by the great sneering creepers. Sunlit birds
yakkety yak above our own deep gloom,
hundreds of feet over our inadequate heads.

How did they do it? We see the marks on trees
but made by what? teeth, weapons, little axes.
They don't communicate except to grin.
We know they're there but jungles grow so fast
and all we have are bruised and bleeding hands.

Classical Disasters

The brazen bull was filled with his bellowing.

The wax was melting as the wings climbed higher.

At the big banquet the food was human.

The greedy cloth bit at his muscular body.

He clubbed the old man at the lonely crossroads.

They cut the tongue from her squealing struggles.

At the last strained heave the stone toppled backwards.

Lines of History

By a deserted road the Apostles were peeing.

The sun through the burning-glass tickled the warm hay.

The sea heaved with its burden of whales.

The antheap was teeming with cries of injustice.

Above the wineshop she cupped her hands and held him.

Past the window of the torture chamber flew the pigeons.

There was no silence, now or at any time.

The Statements

Arts are actually anthropomorphic.
Business is often bilaterally baleful.
Causality is a considerable cow.
Desires are delightful as well as desperate.
Energy in everything is everlasting.
Freedom is frequently fairly fallacious.
Growing girls go gay with gallantry.
History has some horrible hermits.
Illness is injurious only to idiots.
Jokes are jealous and jazz is jolly.
Kitchens are kinetic like kisses and kiwis.
Love is laudable and lately laundered.
Matrimony is mainly merry and miserable.
Names are numinous and never negligible.
Officers often open their orifices.
Palaeontology is particularly painful.
Quails are queer but quiet and queenly.
Restless rovers are rarely repentant.
Soles slide sideways in silent seas.
Terrible tornadoes torture the terrain.
Under umbrellas the uncles take umbrage.
Various virgins veer into vinegar.
Weary wallflowers wait wetly for wisdom.
Xylophones excel in extemporization.
Yelling in youth is yesterday's yawning.
Zen is as zealous as zebras and zinc.

GAVIN EWART

The Headlines

No dice, as Rasputin flies in to floozies

Mean famine tempts 5 bits from Queen

Profs flee as city falls to Turks

Agitator executed on funereal hill

Limeys and krauts combine to flog the frogs

Sage corrupts youth, say City Fathers

Too much water spoils the tea

Norman Archer catches Harold's eye

Demagogue roasts books, heebs

Daughters claim Pop unfit to rule

Allies victorious, fry Troy by stratagem

Short Story

She bit his love-nuts, what a nasty girl!

Her two were always going before her
a perfect pair, so softly supported.

They met in a bar and he was explaining
how 'Baa, Baa, Black Sheep!' is about pubic hair
and how the clitoris is only really
the little boy who lived down the lane.

Stand in front of the mirror and let me lick you.

It was hot on the beach. Too many bikinis
and several hangovers were stretched out in the sun.

They drank a very cold white wine. It
was a great life. After a big lunch
they rolled about on a 42 square foot bed.
Some sand grated into their copulations.

There's a whole literature of the Mediterranean.

He and She and a sea that is tideless
and peaches that ought to be wearing frilly panties.

He was called Jan and she was called Paula.
The Loves were laughing when they got together,
they parted with a shrill cry and a strong backhand
that reddened with a line her bloated floaters.

Xmas for the Boys

A clockwork skating Wordsworth on the ice,
An automatic sermonizing Donne,
A brawling Marlowe shaking out the dice,
A male but metaphysical Thom Gunn.
Get them all now – the latest greatest set
Of all the Poets, dry to sopping wet.

A mad, ferocious, disappointed Swift
Being beaten by a servant in the dark.
Eliot going up to Heaven in a lift,
Shelley going overboard, just for a lark.
Although the tempo and the talent varies
Now is the time to order the whole series.

An electronic Milton, blind as a bat,
A blood-spitting consumptive Keats,
Tennyson calmly raising a tall hat,
Swinburne being whipped in certain dark back streets.
All working models, correct from head to toe –
But Shakespeare's extra, as you ought to know.

Thriller

I drove the hearse back at 70 m.p.h.

My worries flew away, a flock of black birds.
Some shots of rye and on to see Diane.
Complete release. Her legs locked round my back.

But that night wasn't so easy –
there's nothing easy about any money –
I mailed the ransom note and marked the tree.

For two more nights the fuzz was circling badly.
Killing the headlights. From my hide I saw
a fat pockmarked man, with the binocs.

As in the wood he brutishly waited, freezing,
I thought of shallow graves and how the boy
had cried all night about a teddy bear.

But finally I did it with a cushion
and half a bottle of Scotch. Buried him too.
My nerves were bad, the hearse was catching up.

At last the tin box with the elastic band,
nobody there but me. And if the notes were known?
Diane was threshing about, mad at my failure.

Isn't it marvellous how it all turns sour?
Money to burn and burning's all it's fit for,
and down the long black road I drive the hearse.

GAVIN EWART

The Day of the Creator

After a first-rate breakfast I sit in my shirtsleeves
and begin work on my new long poem 'Yelling for Elspeth'.
It's a complicated story full of repetitions,
about a scattering, a dispersion, a diaspora.
It's a love story too and my writing grows curly
as it lingers over the details of that seduction
in the dark bean swamp. Outside my window
the birds are singing a page out of Livy.

Only one could climb the mountain, that is the essence.
The rest were led aside by trolls, their legs jerked like billy-o
as they sank in the viscous mud by the pathside.
I feel I am being split down the middle by an axe
and down the fissure runs the telltale of narrative,
in not too long I shall be as famous as a novelist,
sign copies in bookshops. Down in the garden
a cat is playing god to several sparrows.

I go into the kitchen for a cup of instant coffee,
not too much sugar because of my waistline.
In the cheroot smoke I sort out some characters.
Jacqueline must be like H, and the tall Rabbi
must tell the truth about life to Adrian Semester.
Will Fontainebleau make it? The sugar lumps ponder,
white in blue cardboard. All things are thinkers,
and an ant zigs quietly over the windowsill.

So undisturbed, though I deal with disturbances!
I really have created the pen and the paper.
To the nastiest characters I assign action,
the nice ones sit still in a quiet contemplation.

What colours shall they wear? Would a dialect comic
destroy the whole effect of the nineteenth Canto?
Or improve it? Or what? It's my typewriter
that glints so much knowledge of communication.

Though I write so many words, one thing is certain.
Nobody will shout 'Christ!' at a critical juncture,
there will be no obscenity of thought or deed or even
any long mention of anyone's knickers.
There's a great deal of morality in quietness
and a pure style belongs to a clear sunny morning
and the myth I am holding. Ever so gently
a little white cloud floats over the treetops.

At the lawnmower's purr I stop for a moment.
Would Alaric do anything truly despicable?
Yet when that mean action flowed out of my biro
it seemed somehow so right, so *natural*.
Soon I shall have lunch, then a walk on the Common.
Any sort of exercise is good for my diction
and always has been. That rough dog barking
is like a caesura in my line of neatness.

A Black Rabbit Dies for its Country

Born in the lab, I never saw the grass
or felt the direct touch of wind or sun
and if a rabbit's nature is to run
free on the earth, I missed it; though the glass
never let shot or eager predators pass,

while I was warm against my mother's side
something was waiting in the centrifuge
(the world's a cage, although that cage is huge)
and separate I lived until I died –
watered and fed, I didn't fret, inside,

and all the time was waiting for the paste
scooped with a spatula from the metal rim,
the concentrate bacillus at the brim,
and lived the life of feeling and of taste.
I didn't know it. Knowing would be waste

in any case, and anthrax is the hard
stuff that knocks out the mice, the dogs, the men,
you haven't any chance at all and when
they've finished with you, you're down on a card.
How could I know, to be upon my guard

when they pushed my container into line
with the infected airstream? Breath is life:
though something there more deadly than a knife
cut into me, I was still feeling fine
and never guessed the next death would be mine –

how many minutes later lungs would choke
as feet beat out the seconds like a drum,
hands held me on the table; this was a sum
with the predictable ending of a joke.
Fighting I died, and no god even spoke.

The Pseudo-Demetrius*

After the summer on the lovely island
came the pretender, the autumn of the city,
the Pseudo-Demetrius garlanded with blackberries;
the true young ones had strawberries and raspberries
and the real love in the matchless bed.

After the moistness of the pink lips opening
came the equivocal, the Pseudo-Demetrius,
the one who told us he would make us equal
to what we were when the flowers were young ones
and we knew love in the matchless bed.

After the sun's hour, the failing succession
came with a turbulence but no tenderness,
the anger and envy of the Pseudo-Demetrius,
the one who stirred up trouble and caused the ending
of our best love in the matchless bed.

After the green and the bees in clover
came the new season when we were forgotten,
the riot and sadness of the Pseudo-Demetrius,
brown leaves falling on the musclemen fighting,
and no real love in the matchless bed.

After the summer, after the sun's hour,
came the equivocal, turbulent pretender,
the Pseudo-Demetrius garlanded with autumn,
with lies and fighting in the darkened city,
and death, not love, in the matchless bed.

* In the history of medieval Russia there are two Pretenders.
They are called Pseudo-Demetrius I and Pseudo-Demetrius II.

Abelam

The long-yams are being grown in honour of the moon
A critic recalls Plissetskaya's celebrated jump
Soman is somewhere in the worship of the deadly
The strikers show clever running off the ball
That harpsichord remembers Michael Haydn.

The rainbow, they say, is a snake of no importance
The audience is kinky about Khachaturian
A headline says Hendon Afternoon Dogs
Some secretaries regard themselves as debs
Caroline Quoin on Candlewick has a clear round.

The hornbill carvings are definitely phallic
Graveney is stroking the ball through the covers
A broken choirboy miscalculates some trills
Menstruating women are put in special huts
Blake is accused as a formless draughtsman.

At important ceremonies there are palm-leaf flares
The Porsches like a plague overrun the country
Some minds are tickled by the feathers of investiture
The gin is jumping from the bankers' fountains
The massed choirs are singing A.M.D.G.

The Challenge to Interpretation

Deleterious substances
are hopping with energy/
I am severely
monocoque construction/
In the blue saucepan
tempers are rising/
Two sprauncy birds
inhibit the parkway/
The old movie has
a dancer called Laundrette/

Under the mistletoe
X-rays are working/
At the small breakfast
the bigness of music/
The men in the fields
containers for earthworms/
It is incredible
the smell of the fish-lake/
Je n'aime pas
le *spunk* dans ma bouche/

Crown us
all tenderly/
There are no
differences/
A black dog
is barking/
Love to
the Apostolate/
Goodbye
for ever!

People Will Say We're in Love

But seriously, as the marriage wears on, thanks for the mem-
ory of hauling prams and shopping up icy door-
steps, equally as for the kisses and the dem-
onstrative eyes. Wives work hard. Cathy and her moor-
land romance are fine in the mind, but the car-
ing for babies is the real and most test-
ing fact of a union. The children are the shar-
ing. It's always Housewives *v.* The Rest.

And it's always into big offices for the good provid-
ers, the traditional way to keep the bank man-
agers happy. Families don't like outsid-
ers. This is men's washing and ironing, fan-
ning up a little flame of money in the current acc-
ount. Chores of the typewriter. Essential read-
ing about Management. Not the true sweetness, sacc-
harine at best – a businessman's Creed.

So the success of a marriage can be seen in the chil-
dren and, believe me, certainly yours is the cred-
it, after the nappies, the orange juice, the pil-
fered hours of sleep they took from you, bed-
time too often a night shift, and lov-
ing not the novelist's outspoken rand-
y young sprawlers, pushing and shov-
ing, but tiredness, the offered and the taken hand.

Victorian

Miss with the vapours.
The claret and the oysters.
The curling papers.
Fat clergy in the cloisters.

Heavy squires hunting.
Pints of port and porter.
Grumbling and grunting.
Gothic bricks and mortar.

Fog in the dockyards.
Decorum at the Palace.
Blood in the stockyards.
Murder in the alleys.

The Sentimental Education

Wear your Thomas Hardy suit and sit with candles in the gloom.
Summon ghosts of years departed till they fill the empty room.

First of all call up the weather – heatwave 1922,
Wartime winters with the blackout, blossom on the trees at Kew.

Then the people. First, a nanny. Next, your father wearing spats.
Mummy with her pearls at evening, and her three amazing cats.

Childish captions fit the pictures – you were very childish then –
But you see it still as clearly as the present world of men.

Peter Pan was pulsing drama, green lights shone on Captain Hook.
Carroll's Jabberwock caused nightmares, till you had to hide the book.

You were one. Then came two sisters. They were different from you.
You liked best fried bread and cocoa, loved the zebras at the Zoo.

Then the schools – a bourgeois saga – we all know what they were like.
Minnows in a pond, a bully swam among them like a pike.

Squeeze them in? You'd need a ballroom. Still remembered, many
    names
Cluster round in shorts and sweaters. Latin, algebra and games.

Chapel services. Then freedom, and the length of King's Parade.
Dadie, Anthony – and Classics, all the dons that had it made.

Cicero made ghastly speeches, elegiacs were a bore.
You had two years in the saltmines – how could you come up for more?

Next was English, Richards lectures, Leavis supervising. Fine.
English literature went down as stimulating as new wine.

After Cambridge – unemployment. No one wanted much to know.
Good degrees are good for nothing in the business world below.

In the end you were a salesman, selling lithographic prints.
Trade was stagnant after Munich. Hitler frightened us with hints.

War came down, a blackout curtain, shutting out the kindly sun.
Jews went under, all the playboys somehow lost their sense of fun.

Still, we always had the weather – freezing cold or hot as hell –
Birds continued, flowers were rampant, life went on through shot and
    shell.

Back at last to shabby London, tired and rationed, sad to see,
With its tales of air raid wardens, siren suits and hot sweet tea.

People, literary people, now replaced the roaring boys
Fond of vino, signorinas, dirty jokes and lots of noise.

Tambi, Nicholas and Helen. Come on in. You see them plain.
Publishing will never, surely, be as odd as that again.

Money, said the British Council, I have money in my hand.
Get your hair cut, keep your nose clean, live in Civil Serviceland.

Six years later came the end game – middle grades were axed. Goodbye!
They were victims of the Beaver's petulant persistent cry.

Advertising. Advertising. Fatal Lady of the Lake!
No one opts for copywriting, they get in there by mistake.

You absorbed those business ethics – not the Sermon on the Mount –
Walked into that artful parlour, had the William Hill account.

Let the room explode with whizz kids, dollies, every kind of Pop!
Only crematorium silence brings that mayhem to a stop.

Money. Children. Mortgage. Rat race. Anxious words that tax the brain.
Nagging fears of unemployment drive the middle class insane.

It's not pretty when they throw you, screaming, in the empty sack,
Filled with nothing but the cries of wives and children screaming back.

Does the working class get ulcers? No one worries much, if so.
They know jobs are hard to come by, and the pay is often low.

They're inured to thoughts of hardship and of being out of work.
This is life. It's no good blubbing, throwing fits or going berserk.

Moneyed men in Lloyds, the City, can't imagine what it's like.
To the driver of an E-type, what's the old penurious bike?

Workmen are a bloody nuisance – just a ROAD UP sign or two –
Obstacles that spoil their record from the Bank to Luton Hoo.

Keep your voice down. Don't start shouting. Let the candles burn up
    straight.
(Privileged and trendy diners stuff themselves with After Eight.)

All you learn – and from a lifetime – is that that's the way it goes.
That's the crumbling of the cookie, till the turning up of toes.

Dean Swift Watches Some Cows

How, when they lift their Tails, the Shit shoots out!
A foul Volcanoe next a Waterspout.
The Anus and Vagina are so near,
Each lovely Dame cannot repress a Tear
To think she's modelled on the selfsame Pattern.
And so are Queens, and so is ev'ry Slattern.

'Twas the Propinquity of these two Holes
That made Divines doubt Women had not Souls.
They knew those Furrows that would bear the Tilth –
Men could not choose but sow their Seed in Filth –
And how from Ordure sprung could Life be good
Or Mystery be part of Womanhood?

From the Phrase Book

Surely it is only right to arrive
With a satisfactory sausage for Germaine?

He is very sick, he has taken an overdraft.
The label tells: Pour in two heaping teaspoons.

There is something wrong with my transmission.
I was slightly oiled at the Service Station.

Did you not buy it for two hundred florins?
You will not get much change out of him.

In this country it is not politic to talk
But our new prison is the best in the world.

Drive to the left, Sir, and take the motorway.
That is the fastest road to the Cemetery.

Fiction: The Definite Article

What was the mood? Calm. What was the
    weather? Rainy. He crumbed the
kitchen table with his hands, felt the
    caster sugar sandy on fingers, the
milkblots wet. Across the road the
    sign of the Blue Star Garage, the
blue and white letters, showed. The
    B and the S were obscured, the
message LUE TAR; if he moved the
    extra foot or so one way the
words became UE AR. He called it the
    message of continued existence, the
Great Affirmation, even the
    gateway had blocked the
words for its own purpose. This was the
    trumpeted identity, the

tall fact of heness; and the
    effect was to make him all the
more lonely. Each morning he woke with the
    cry: 'Darling!', with the
languid 'You made me stiff!', the
    hangover of old love, the
memory of big bosoms, the
    carbon copy of youth, the
result of education. Oh, the
    loneliness! Bland in the
huge city, he meditated the
    others; they moved the
legs and arms, they were the
    working clockwork models, the
human scenery his eye walked past, the
    tribes perfected in the sign of 'the'.

Fiction: A Message

'My dear fellow!' said the great poet, putting his arm affably
                     round Ponsonby's neck,
'I respect your feelings for Gertrude. I realize they have something
                     to do with sec
or secs or whatever they call it. Of course in my little backwater I
                     haven't moved with the times –
just listen to the bells of St Josef – how I love those chimes!'

Down below, the Austrian lake reflected his agonized incomprehension
                     sleepily in the sun.
'I'm at the end of my tether!' cried Ponsonby. 'But you –
                     your race is nearly run –
I look to you for a message. I know that behind her spectacles she
                     has the most beautiful eyes,
I've heard her playing Chopin at midnight with rapt, adoring cries!'

'These things are sent to try us,' said Anzeiger. 'You'll find something
                     in Apollonius of Rhodes
or one of the Desert Fathers, that proves fairly conclusively that
                     women are toads.'
'I've told myself so, yet I often have the most incomprehensible
                     puzzling dreams.
I dream of the Kaiserhof, of milk churns, of chocolate creams.

Sometimes I run into a dark wood of feathery soft perfumed
                     aromatic trees
or I'm sinking in unimaginable sweetness like honey, right
                     up to my knees,
or I see Gertrude waving from a cottage with a very attractive
                     rose-circled door.
I'm wearing my Norfolk jacket and, I'm ashamed to say, nothing more!

'That sounds like the Flesh,' pondered Anzeiger, fingering gently
                     Ponsonby's fair curls.

'We know well that St Anthony was tempted in dreams by demons
                                   and dancing girls.
Though these apparitions, old fellow, seem so irrational, so disturbing,
                                   so unaccountably odd,
I think we can safely assume, in your case, they don't come from God.

Though, of course, He has been known to work in some really very
                                   mysterious ways.'
'But what shall I do?' cried Ponsonby. 'Offer it up. Just
                                   pray and give praise.
We'll take the pony and trap and go down on Sunday, dear boy,
                                   to Linz.
The Lord will lend a kindly ear to your account of your sins.'

They turned and walked towards the house, arm in arm. The sun
                                   had nearly set.
As they approached the pretty garden, by the last dark sentinel
                                   pine trees they met
Gertrude in a light summer dress, confidently smiling, friendly
                                   and demure.
Ponsonby smiled back. He was above her. Of that he was now sure.

Fiction: The House Party

Ambrose is an Old Etonian and he
is terribly in love with a girl called Fluffy
who has Lesbian tendencies and is very attracted
to a sophisticated debutante called Angela Fondling
who was once the mistress of old Lord Vintage.

Don and Vi come to stay at The Castle
and neither of them know how looking-glasses aren't mirrors
or what wines go best with fish or even how to
handle a butter knife or talk about horses.
Don makes a joke about being unstable.

Fluffy doesn't know where to look and Ambrose
chokes on his claret. His Lordship is thinking
about a certain incident in 1930
when 'Filthy' Fynes-Pantlebury rode a bay gelding
up the main staircase and into a bathroom.

Angela is writing a book about the middle classes,
she keeps giving Don and Vi gin and depth interviews
and trying like a mad thing to understand Bradford.
Lady Vintage is pathetically faded
but she loves a young criminal in London: Reg. Ratcock.

They sometimes meet in the afternoon, on Fridays,
and smoke a lot of pot in the tenement basement.
Ambrose is thinking of taking Holy Orders,
he usually thinks of Fluffy as a very young choirboy.
Vi wants to go to the loo but she's shy about asking.

Lord Vintage has vanished into several daydreams;
he remembers well how Frank Fondling once shot a beater.
Don is getting very tired of gin. Vi wets her knickers.
Fluffy says to Ambrose: 'But what *is* a chasuble?'
And Angela keeps her tape-recorder running . . .

Experience Hotel

The alcoholically inclined
who live in this hotel
are often stoned out of their mind
and only ring the bell
for bottles of that special kind
they know and love so well.

The ladies in their mules and wraps
who haunt the corridors
are knowledgeable about Dutch caps
and more discreet than whores
though not so different perhaps
behind their numbered doors.

The staff is neutral in all this
and tired by too much work
ignoring every pinch and kiss
from drunks who slyly lurk
to grope the matron and the miss
and the Manhattan clerk.

The Larkin Automatic Car Wash

Back from the Palace of a famous king,
  Italian art
Making the roped-off rooms a Culture thing,
At about five o'clock we made a start,
Six teenagers squashed in. And as I drove
North from the barley sugar chimney pots
They sang the changeable teenager songs
That fade like tapestries those craftsmen wove,
But centuries more quickly. Through the knots
Of road-crossing pedestrians, through the longs

And shorts of planners' morse, the traffic lights,
  Over a hill,
Down to the garage advertising tights,
A special bargain, fast I drove on till
I drew up by the new Car Wash machine,
Pride of the forecourt, where a sign said STOP
Clear on the asphalt. In front a smaller car
Stood patiently as brushes swooshed it clean,
Whirling its streaming sides and back and top –
A travelling gantry; verticals, cross-bar.

We wound our windows up and waited there.
  In pixie green
The moving monster lifted itself clear,
The yellow brushes furled and now were seen
As plastic Christmas trees. Its wet last client
Made for the highway and it was our turn.
In gear and under. Two tenpences fed in
A slot on the driver's side. The pliant
Great brushes whirred and closed. Like yellow fern
One blurred the windscreen. Underwater thin

The Science Fiction light came creeping through
    Alien and weird
As when the vegetables invade in *Dr Who*,
Something to be amused at – almost, feared.
And as the lateral brushes closed our sides,
Sweeping past steadily back, the illusion came
That *we* were moving forward; and I checked
The hard-on handbrake, thought of switchback rides
And how the effect in childhood was the same –
Momentary fear that gathered, to collect

In joy of safety. The tall half-children screamed –
    The girls at least –
Delighted to be frightened, as it seemed,
By this mechanical otherworldly beast.
The boys made usual, window-opening, jokes.
And soon, tide-turning, the brushes travelled back,
Put our imagination in reverse,
Though we were still. Like cigarettes and cokes
This was their slight excitement, took up slack
In time that wound by, idle. Nothing worse

And nothing better. To me it seemed so short,
    I wanted more,
I wanted hours, I wanted to be caught
In that wet undergrowth by that wet shore.
This was an exit from our boring life,
A changed environment, another place,
A hideout from the searchers. Otherness
Was that world's commonplace, a kitchen knife,
Something so usual that it had no face –
As the car dripped unnatural cleanliness.

Yes, it was jolly, *Fun for the kids* we say,
   But more than that;
For if you look at it another way
This was a notable peak where all is flat.
Into the main road by the riverside
We right-turned past the pubs that line the route
Where cheering crowds watch boat race crews go by,
Travelling with the full incoming tide.
The roof, the sides, the bonnet and the boot
Shone with new wetness. Yet the dust could lie

As thick there as before; and would, in time,
   This was reprieve.
Cars too grow old and dirty. Gin-and-lime
Perks up the guest; but all guests have to leave.
In through the main gate of the block of flats
I drove my giggling adolescent load,
And in vibrating door-slammed solitude
I parked. Under their different hats
Spiritual experiences work in a kind of code.
Did I have one? I, from this multitude?

ZULFIKAR GHOSE

The Body's Independence

1

Father Bianchi taught biology
in Bombay's Don Bosco High School, but skipped
the parts I had learned about already.
The classroom beamed faces, keen and tight-lipped,
bare brown arms on desks, fingers steady.

His white cassock arm-sleeves rolled against heat,
the Father went through the motions of the body
with a cane to point at a chart and hit
on our heads. His voice, a lesson in prosody,
told us of the secrets of the heart.

He demonstrated man, the button at his throat
loose: he described in the air, with his cane,
the nervous system, showed how the brain was alert.
We furtively laughed at the shape of man,
but his eyes saw further than the chart.

2

A hawk stood high above Malabar Hill,
watching the whole island. In the afternoon's
sun-stunned silence a coconut fell.
A dog, his skin vibrating over bones
to rid him of flies, barked. And I fell ill:

kidney haemorrhage that oozed blood
into the bladder. I felt the hawk's beak
pull at a kidney, like a worm out of mud,
as my skin shrank and tightened over the weak
skeleton. All the pains the heart withstood,

and did not fall. A kind woman by my bed
kept vigil, telling a favourite tale:
how Babur, the Mogul King, prayed and tried
to bring back his son to life and grew pale
himself with Humayun's illness and died.

But Humayun had lived to rule. She said
a whole kingdom waited to see me crowned,
with the oil of life to anoint my head.
My body took shape like the chart, I found
the outline of bones fill with flesh and blood.

3

A crow shifted from his nest to a branch,
pulled his black tongue at the sun and let fall
a splotch of white into the shade. A finch
flew out. The crow laughed. An eagle, appalled,
moved to another tree. A snake looked, flinched.

India was at civil war,
the crow excreted where he pleased. And I,
reborn from a fairy-tale, saw bones charred
in mounds on pavements. It was no country
for princes, and the eagle soared

above the darker clouds. The undergrowth
heaved uneasily with poison of snakes.
'The heart is free!' people cried. 'What if truth
runs out like blood? We have our independence.'
The blood of India ran out with my youth.

The Mystique of Roots

1

Eagles, coupling in the air, are still
wings cushioned on floating dust.
Roadside houses are bowls
in which peasants knead bread out of dust. Dust
rises from the farmer's plough. He sows dust.
The long arm of the sun wipes India's brow.
I lie coughing all afternoon.
The sun breaks through the window-pane like a stone,
crashing its fragments of light on my face.
The beam of dust in the room is my throat.
My gullet is air through which eagles fall.
India makes me breathless.

2

The fields are yellow with mustard-seed plant.
I lie flat as a lizard in the clover.
The sun moves up my neck like an ant.
But who is this woman calls me lover?

Where a eucalyptus tree's branches thin
into the sky, hawks seem still as they cover
miles, simply floating. I cannot begin
to love this woman who calls me lover.

The mystique of roots worries me. I rise,
step firmly on the earth, kick at clover,
pluck mustard flowers. There is no end to cries
that call me over and over and over.

3

Where can one go in a country so large?
Hawks fly at a tangent to the earth's curve.
I do not have the language that could serve
me in such loneliness. The stiff plumage
of eagles does not falter at heights where
they float, insensible to the sweet air
that I would breathe. For these roots in their crust
of earth carry worms. What I breathe is dust.

Flying over India

The point of the eagle's introspection
or its lonely watch-tower withdrawal
is also my point of view. This crab-crawl
flight through sand-holes of air and the suction
of blue, blue, blue makes the jungle below
seem a rotation-crops plot grown fallow;

nothing moves in the relativity
of speed. India lies still in primeval
intactness of growth. The great alluvial
plains are sodden with trees: neither city
nor village intrudes with temples and towers
in this sprawling virgin-land decked with flowers

and trees, trees. At the jungle's edge, a river
coils out to shed its snake-skin waters to the charm
of the sea. The bizarre, purposeless calm
of sand, the country's dangerous cobra-glitter!
The jet rises up in the ocean-swell
of the sky and slides through the air like a shell.

The pilot announces famous landmarks.
But what sand-dune civilization sank
in the mud-banks, what mosquito-kingdom drank
up the healing waters? The spoilt monarchs
of luxurious empires could not prevent
the bush-fires of religious dissent.

Give me the purer air. The flat earth is awful.
Give me height, height, with its cold perspective
of forms of the earth. Senseless now to dive
like eagles to the earth's sparrows. The jungle's
beasts are unseen from here. From these heights,
one can almost believe in human rights.

This Landscape, These People

I

My eighth spring in England I walk among
   the silver birches of Putney Heath,
   stepping over twigs and stones: being stranger,
   I see but do not touch: only the earth
   permits an attachment. I do not wish
to be seen, and move, eyes at my sides, like a fish.

And do they notice me, I wonder, these
   Englishmen strolling with stiff country strides?
   I lean against a tree, my eyes are knots
   in its bark, my skin the wrinkles in its sides.
   I leap hedges, duck under chestnut boughs,
and through the black clay let my swift heels trail like ploughs.

A child at a museum, England for me
   is an exhibit within a glass case.
   The country, like an antique chair, has a rope
   across it. I may not sit, only pace
   its frontiers. I slip through ponds, jump ditches,
through galleries of ferns see England in pictures.

2

My seventeen years in India I swam
   along the silver beaches of Bombay,
   pulled coconuts from the sky, and tramped
   red horizons with the swagger and sway
   of Romantic youth; with the impudence
of a native tongue, I cried for independence.

A troupe came to town, marched through villages;
   began with two tight-rope walkers, eyes gay
   and bamboos and rope on their bare shoulders;
   a snake charmer joined them, beard long and grey,
   baskets of cobras on his turbaned head;
through villages marched: children, beating on drums, led

them from village to village, and jugglers
   joined them and swallowers of swords, eaters
   of fire brandishing flames through the thick air,
   jesters with tongues obscene as crows', creatures
   of the earth: stray dogs, lean jackals, a cow;
stamping, shouting, entertaining, making a row

from village to village they marched to town:
   conjurers to bake bread out of earth, poets
   to recite epics at night. The troupe, grown
   into a nation, halted, squirmed: the sets
   for its act, though improvised, were re-cast
from the frames of an antique, slow-moving, dead past.

India halted: as suddenly as a dog,
   barking, hangs out his tongue, stifles his cry.
   An epic turned into a monologue
   of death. The rope lay stiff across the country;
   all fires were eaten, swallowed all the swords;
the horizons paled, then thickened, blackened with crows.

Born to this continent, all was mine
   to pluck and taste: pomegranates to purple
   my tongue and chillies to burn my mouth. Stones
   were there to kick. This landscape, these people –
   bound by the rope, consumed by their fire.
Born here, among these people, I was a stranger.

3

This landscape, these people! Silver birches
   with polished trunks chalked around a chestnut.
   All is fall-of-night still. No thrush reaches
   into the earth for worms, nor pulls at the root
   of a crocus. Dogs have led their masters home.
I stroll, head bowed, hearing only the sound of loam

at my heel's touch. Now I am intimate
   with England; we meet, secret as lovers.
   I pluck leaves and speak into the air's mouth;
   as a woman's hair, I deck with flowers
   the willow's branches; I sit by the pond,
my eyes are stars in its stillness; as with a wand,

I stir the water with a finger until
   it tosses waves, until countries appear
   from its dark bed: the road from Putney Hill
   runs across oceans into the harbour
   of Bombay. To this country I have come.
Stranger or an inhabitant, this is my home.

Poem Towards Sanity

Take them away. I have seen a pear split
just lying in a basket; whole breakfast
rooms of insidious sounds – the fridge
silent as snow, gas-flames dry as cactus,
and the insect growths, all quietly bridge
inarticulate space – compel a spirit,
give substance to nothing, a silly cut,
a razor slash on the cheek of a fruit.

It is to be doubted that anyone's
mind has mountains. Silences certainly
without which no chasms are possible;
and echoing of words which urbanely
proffer the grosser notions – that a table
is also a cosmos with moons and suns.
Who can take them away? My nose runs.
My eyes are gluey as currants.

How a giddiness unsteadies my hand
as I shave! Soapsuds twinkle in my eyes
and explode loudly. I slice their mellow
roundness. My lathered cheek is scratched like glass.
Something moves. A shape, an idea, a glow
in the eye? A falsification of hind-
sight: that the indivisible wholeness
of an atom also bounds the flight of sounds.

The mid-February cries of birds are mad.
A car gurgles with its run-down battery.
Water streaming down a florist's window
makes a gesture of spring. An artery

of blood, thick as a tulip, booms with a slow
deliberation. I walk. I walk. Amid
the wicker-work heath's wintry enclosures
I listen for a final explosion.

Mutability

Not even the trees. The tallest plane-trees
in Hyde Park seem cartographers' smudged marks
on an old map of London, hardly these
survivors of elaborate road-works.
How the concrete rises against the sky!
This air also has the finality
of abstraction: observe the water crease –
as if a horse's tail swished at a fly,

so little movement. All landscapes dissolve
no sooner than they seem memorable.
I shut my eyes on faces which I love
to make finer sensations possible:
mutability can appear absurd
when memory keeps an exact record.
And yet at times I too feel disabled,
forget a face or an important word.

Nothing really holds. Jets unlock their wheels
descending over London in a suspense
of diminishing motion. God, what it feels
like to be coming to a stop, or to sense
that one is never going to be the same!
The tall trees bewilder me with their calm.
To abstract from life a permanence
is art's process to which life has no claim.

Marriages

1

Go to your marriages, sisters, my own
bachelorhood falls from me as an acorn
among the oak's roots. I drive you slowly
to Liverpool and concentrate wholly
on driving. You sleep, tired of England's
fields. You are going. Go, sisters, to husbands,
children; your lives are expectations which
your beauty will realize and enrich.

2

What can a brother say, what advice give?
Occasions of this sort we come to live
with, expect: partings, deaths accumulate.
To love despite absences is to relate
substance and form to belief. Forgive
me. I give you abstractions when you leave
the real experience of love with me,
your gift. I generalize from memory.

3

Mid-March in England is breaking new ground,
bursting with trees; once more spring has come round,
and I find it harder than ever not to be
sentimental. I should have been a tree.
I belong to this landscape but not to these
people. I am a birch by a pool that marries
its own reflection. How then can I bring
myself to your marriages this English spring?

4

I remain alone now that you are going;
now, as in a landscape where it is snowing,
though I stand in need of warmth, love, I withdraw
to myself with a tree's isolation; before
me the landscape thins to the dust I breathe.
I see a woman whom I love recede
to the horizon. You go. What have I lost?
My mind is heavy with words, my limbs with frost.

Friends

My friends are charitable, kind,
men of good bearing, humour.
One lends his money, one his mind,
whichever they have, less or more,
to my pursuit of poetry.
I grow in their wood, a plain tree.

I drink up their words and their cash
as so much rain or songs of birds;
I am lime and maple, chestnut, ash,
bending in their meadows where herds
of their laughter continually pass.
I listen, nod, and tip my glass.

I say little and offer less;
unshaved often and out of fags,
a crooked nose and hair in mess,
my morose-Ghose face empties bags
of silence to their packets of crisps.
A waiter, I collect their tips.

Alone, I remember them, and
recall each generosity.
Drunk or sober, I understand
their love is the root of all poetry.
Kind, charitable, since they are both,
I am evergreen in my growth.

The Water-Carrier

A man the colour of dry earth, a stone
tied to the air with a loin-cloth, carries
his goatskin bag of water like an oversize
wart permanently growing from his back:

a floating oasis in the Saharas
of thirst, the liquid shadow of a palm-tree:
the water-carrier slips through the empty
afternoon streets like an underground stream.

Where the sun drives him like a mule
towards the troughs of the horizon's haze.
And the stars at night which are also always
maddeningly hot like the eyes of women.

Quite in order, then, that man should be
an itinerant element, a water
cloud moving over the earth, his feet on fire
as they nibble the desert sands:

even if after his long-distance haul
the water-carrier finds his own thirst
the greatest of all, a multi-tongued curse
in the saliva-drouth of unending desert.

An Attachment to the Sun

We sat eating fruit, a tangerine first,
peeling London's frost for a tropical grove:
our convivial attachment to the sun
is also our love.

Suddenly she laughed. A rush of glow-worms
breathed in her eyes. The window, lined with ice,
unbuttoned a row of geraniums
gay as butterflies.

I broke two walnuts in my palm. Lizards
clicked their tongues in her mouth. We tricked
the weather with love, made London a suburb
of the Tropics.

The Crows

Crows will stick their beaks into anything.
Ugliness protects them: children don't care
to pet them, and when they descend on trees,
eagles discreetly go somewhere quieter.

They will sit on balconies and appear
to comment on passing traffic. Their black
cloak never conceals the dagger of speech,
their communal weapon. They talk, talk, talk.

I've heard them break the silence of night
with sudden loud cawing as if provoked
into dispute by a falling star,
and then flying skywards as though to look

up some evidence, keen as scientists;
yet really, when you see their missions
come mostly to nothing, they appear more
like intensely dedicated politicians.

The Incurable Illness

Ron, when I looked up the cricket scores this
morning to see how Pollock was cutting his
way through the county bowlers like a rail-
road across a continent despite this cool
summer, I saw instead the notice
that you'd died at 38. Ron, I felt foul.

It didn't say what the mortal illness was.
Leukaemia or cancer, I suppose,
a tumour or a heart disease that proud science
is humiliated by: there's no sense
in such dying. It just happens: no because
lessens the shock, no text-book explains.

When in successive months four Boeings crashed –
the aluminium crumpled, the instruments dashed
to bits – the death-toll sent the stomach diving.
But we know such things happen: the iced wing
of a plane buckles, the radar screen, washed
spotless as linen by failure, goes blank, nothing

survives. We call it chance, hazard, bad luck.
Calling life a gamble, we've learned to truck
with sudden death, being fatalists when
the cause is recognizable; even
road accidents and train derailments don't shock
sensibility. But to die with some obscure organ

diseased, to be outwardly as perfect
as colour supplement models while some inner defect
gives the lungs or the liver the texture

of timber that's riddled by wood-worm – we're
all riding the empty sky on a faulty jet
if so deceptive is the functioning of nature.

I see Europe raising towers of concrete
and glass and filling forms for the effete
state. The computers are programmed, the pill
marketed. The inventions which permit life also kill;
we're the products we make, congenitally obsolete.
Each one of us is incurably ill.

Ron, I feel foul, remembering your pink face,
your well-cut suit. There was nothing wrong I could
  trace
in your features: no more than in a jet
before take-off or in civilized Europe. And yet,
Ron, and yet. What's happening to our race?
We're dying sooner than we expected.

The Lost Culture

Clouds labour across the sky like goatskin bags
invisibly borne on the mule's back of sooty space.

I drive along the plane-treed avenues of Holland Park
where churches give proportion to the streets.

Boeings descending turn exactly above the corner
of Norland Square: as generations of salmon

return to the same river unfailingly. The Central Line
pumps through an underground stream, quiet as blood.

A man-hole stinks, the guttered earth is sick.
London is mapped in all conceivable dimensions.

I would like to levitate above all this
time-tabled fuss, an eagle with a mobile's

slow-motion fixedness in a tropical sky.
London is an empty lift-shaft in a nightmare.

The Tate has acquired a pink squiggle
on white and grey and is pleased as a disc jockey.

This emptied brown-paper bag of a culture
goes pop, garish as detergent packaging.

Because the beggarwoman on the Bombay pavement
had a leprous skin, scabs for pores

and a pink gloss where the skin was torn;
because the child she led she had herself blinded

to gouge the coins of pity, a fierce
bargain with murderous hunger; not only she,

who chides me now for my foreign words,
for turning from the vernacular of hunger,

dropped the earthen begging-bowl of culture
in fragments at my feet, cruel India.

London is a power-failure in my head. Asoka's
wheel makes souvenir-pottery out of my brain.

I am an old eagle, moulting.
My music is hybrid jazz of no tradition.

One Chooses a Language

1

The memorial to Petrarch is plain
at Fontaine de Vaucluse where the mountain
still dominates the waters it lets run
from its mouth. In English, French and German,
slot-machines relate the history of
the place and its poet and his mad love.
One chooses a language, puts in a coin,
and understands. It's cheap and to the point.

2

The English alphabet dangled its *A*
for Apple when I was eight in Bombay.
I stuttered and chewed almonds for a cure.
My tongue, rejecting a vernacular
for a new language, resisted utterance.
Alone, I imitated the accents
of English soldiers, their pitch and their tone.
They were the mouths to my tongue's microphone.

3

The wind turned the houses inside out at
Gordes, but why is Les Baux so desolate?
The weather, or commercial demands, change:
the people go elsewhere, learn a strange
tongue to make a new living; refugees
all from want. I'm a tourist among these
ruins. My Michelin Guide in hand,
I read about this earth and understand.

4

Back on the ferry, connecting two shores,
on the stateless sea among anecdotes
and duty-free liquor, I've nothing to say
who said little between Dunkirk and Marseille.
There's England, my dictionary my ignorance
brings me back to. I give poetry readings
where people ask at the end (just to show
their interest) how many Indian languages I know.

A Short History of India

Ever since Asoka's wheel advertised
the endless potential of endeavour,
the wobbly wheel of the bullock-cart
has ploughed the pumpkin earth.

The people remained earth-banks on the roadside,
idle as rubbish, while the imperial copper
of aggrandizement was hammered out until
the tinkering echoed in the loneliest alley.

Look now at the enfranchised people,
the spoiled votes of a democracy:
passivity can never be ruled,
nor a wheel negotiate a ditch.

The Picnic in Jammu

Uncle Ayub swung me round and round
till the horizon became a rail
banked high upon the Himalayas.
The trees signalled me past. I whistled,
shut my eyes through tunnels of the air.
The family laughed, watching me puff
out my muscles, healthily aggressive.

*This was late summer, before the snows
come to Kashmir, this was picnic time.*

Then, uncoupling me from the sky, he
plunged me into the river, himself
a bough with me dangling at its end.
I went purple as a plum. He reared
back and lowered the branch of his arm
to grandma who swallowed me with a kiss.
Laughter peeled away my goosepimples.

*This was late summer, before the snows
come to Kashmir, this was picnic time.*

After we'd eaten, he aimed grapes at
my mouth. I flung at him the shells of
pomegranates and ran off. He tracked
me down the river-bank. We battled,
melon-rind and apple-core our arms.
'You two!' grandma cried. 'Stop fighting, you'll
tire yourselves to death!' We didn't listen.

*This was late summer, before the snows
come to Kashmir and end children's games.*

Kew Bridge

4.30 over Kew Bridge and the sun
on the wall-like stillness of the river
is broken into dog-roses. These frail
November evenings hold the horizon
for no longer than the bus takes to cross
the bridge. The sky is dogskin whose shiver
casts off droplets of colour. How I fail
daily to make sense of a sense of loss!
My days grow darker earlier than dark
nights can fall. I wake in darkness who sleep
past sunrise. This bridge is a landmark
dividing my day: the work done to keep
me alive, to do the work for which I live.
Dogs are bounding on Kew Green, chasing
a ball and bringing it back. I survive
merely a day's weariness, the weather's mood,
writing a word now and now erasing
a phrase with a weak will's ineptitude
to conserve feeling. I go and come, arrive
home as a dog to his master, the ball
of the spent day sticking in my throat. I
go and come at dayrise and at nightfall
to the same place and at the same time by
the same bus, I go and come, yet always
seem to be here where the traffic slows down.
4.30 over Kew Bridge: yesterday's
dogs begin to bark and tomorrow's sun
is setting: only twenty-four hours disown
me each day. I go and come, go and come:
as if suspended mobility were my home.

A Difficult Child

More proficient than a ventriloquist,
he imitates birdcalls with a shut mouth;
with a conjurer's deftness, he can throw
balls of paper across the class without
moving his hands from the desk. He can spit
bubble-gum so high into the air that
it sticks to the ceiling. Whatever he
does, demands attention. Once he even
lit a cigarette, took a puff, and stubbed
it out in a sudden mime so swiftly
executed that he didn't seem to move
at all, and the whole class applauded him.
Chewing paper, he rolls it on his tongue
and shoots it right into the teacher's ear.
Twelve years ago when chocolates were
rationed and flowers expensive, a young
man gave a girl this bastard. The teacher
wonders what use punishment would be for
one who has never known anything else.

The Pursuit of Frost

Wandering again, come
to this shore, observing the severe
disenchantment of water which remains
    anonymous and clear:
        cleanse what stains
here and trumpet which purity a welcome

    through arches of the mind?
All this and crushed like aluminium cans,
like burnt-out fires a black patch left, smokers'
    lungs on the shore. All runs
        to neglect, to wreckers'
yards goes all where metal-chewing machines grind

    up a culture. Carbon waste,
that's all of the air expelled. A seismograph
needle, that's all, as if gaudy Broadway were granite
    that heaved. But enough, enough.
        Wandering, can it
be as with bird-migrations – to taste

    the warm waters and to move
on always ahead of the cold-front, flying
from the pursuit of frost? What assaults
    landscapes then, conferring
        on evergreens a false
permanence? The eye remembers, does not reprove

    the mind but only feasts
on new possibilities. Here, and here, establish
settlement or dynasty or whatever satisfies

vanity. Have your wish,
    wanderer, for butterflies
will soon go south and the fabulous beasts

    will return to their god-
forsaken mythologies, reviving terror.
Broken glass and fragmented pottery, underground
    cables and what error not on error
        compounded: a lost-and-found
civilization (a home, wanderer!), an ancient fraud.

It's Your Land, Boss

On a hillside in Texas,
digging the brown earth to deliver like calves
the limestone rocks with which it bulged, I thought:
   The stubborn earth survives
      more than the periodic drought
and the seasonal rainstorm; but how affects us

   the word, O Earth, we call,
stooping, when like pilgrims we come to a land,
packaged across the turbulent air in the paths of jets!
   A T.V. feature, canned
      for syndication, that's
the prophet's dramatic way: to come home and fall

   on his knees with an at last
finality, seeing salvation in a handful of earth.
I think of Israel and of the Jews who kill
   and die for it, the land worth
      the idea they fulfil
with their dying, an absolute belief and trust

   that the earth has a mother's
claim to patriotic rites and sacrificial feasts.
The coarse, porous earth, toothy with flints,
   casting out mythological beasts,
      cynically hints
that it might actually be soulless. Let others

   define whose perceptions
don't pickaxe the soil. I have more on my mind.

There's the grave mystique, too, compelling the youth
    of America to find
        primitive versions of truth,
to lose itself in flowery misconceptions,

    wearing homespun cloth and beads;
or to stand before microphones on a college campus
and declare its own peculiar allegiance
    to the earth. And thus,
        whether it makes sense
or not, a revolutionary rhetoric breeds

    a counter-rhetoric's pretentious
slogans: *America – Love It or Leave It,* and so on.
Earth-kissing Zionists aside (and each country
    is an Israel for someone),
        people don't really
care nowadays for sentimental gestures,

    for sacredness is suspect,
the earth more a problem for conservation than
a banner across a jingoist breast, and the land
    merely a real estate speculation.
        Countries, countries! Brand-
names, faded and disfigured, on the wrecked

    product that builds up rust
among the weeds and wild flowers growing high behind
the idle farms. Worms and beetle-like insects
    and the burrowing animals find
        a home in the wreck's
corrugations. Old mother earth's a heap of dust.

My temporary peasant fervour
plays out its fantasy on the Texas hillside.
I'm not sure what this earth means to me.
　　I don't take the peasant's pride
　　　　in the quality
of the soil. I don't need to. But feel poorer

　　because of this loss,
this irrelevance. I rake aside the stones, push
at a rock that's too heavy to move. I throw
　　away tufts of grass. From this lush
　　　　land, too, I must go
towards horizons which the jet-liners cross.

Come, Sailor

Not by journeying,
Odysseus (since to you the Mediterranean's
currents are erratic, violent mysteries),
   not fresh explorations
     now amidst the swollen seas,
Odysseus, will bring back the heart-soothing

   vision, nor will the hills
again be purple near the town that was once
home; and sooner will the extinct birds rise
   in imagined migrations
     before your startled eyes
than your searching discover the particles

   of dust become again
compacted into masonry, the walls and domes
of fallen cities. Open gutters and sewers
   ran out of those kingdoms
     whose golden towers
only are remembered, and the fields of yellow corn

   were sometimes black
with locusts. The hills of Rome, the isles
of Greece, even there, Odysseus. And still,
   when you stand beside the sails
     and look down at the tall
waves shouldering your ship, there, Odysseus, like

   a drowned sailor
a body floats, its face yours and mine. Compulsive,
this voyaging – as if the next calm will settle
   the sea-spray and drive
     away the clouds until
the horizon offers the choice of a natural harbour

where intermingled come
scents of thyme and rosemary, or a clearer
perspective of the ocean's routes, each one
   an illusion that nearer
     is that vision
which makes sons slam doors on their parents' home.

   Chill breezes catalogue
again autumn's severities; the sky hurries eastward
and the gulls ride a swifter wind. The seas
   twitch, and again the voice you heard
     in ancient mythologies
calls: Come, sailor, journey towards the cold fog.

View from the Observatory

Through dark space, measurable
only in light-years, as if penetrating the surface
of an ocean one saw little silver fish glow in a dance
　　and turn the liquid space
　　　　into twinkling fluorescence,
suddenly appeared the distant stars: the visible

　　thus transcends belief,
and the years are reduced to the bleep-bleep
of radio signals. Vega quivered at the centre,
　　turning green and then deep
　　　　blue, not a bright star
at all, but a mass of self-contradiction, a thief

　　of its own identity.
How the years go! Dispersed in space like smoke,
reaching farther than a telescope can retrieve.
　　The distant stars provoke
　　　　a theology: we should believe
more than we see. And yet the recalcitrant naked eye

　　wearily contracts its pupil
from such grey-haired wisdom, seeking only the delight
of surprise. Pocked with craters, the moon appeared,
　　full of October, I thought, bright
　　　　as over the Pacific, smeared
and streaked with sweat. But no, a simple,

　　unpoetical moon, closer
to its own truth, masked with a topography
that veined and hollowed its bloated opulence.

But there's no truth in it if I
    close my eyes, no sense
beyond the starry explosions in the inner

    darkness, none at all,
the sputterings of colour, the delicate flames
which burn the inside of eyelids, the flares
    at their blinding games
        in the charred sockets. There's
wisdom in sudden illuminations! Sparks fall

    from fireworks as easily
as stars from a heaven the astronomer builds
like a pointillist adding more and more dots
    until the stretched space fills
        up and a new perspective creates
a new illusion for which the telescope is busily

    aimed to the precise minute.
We may agree on a world with open eyes but
the rebel years will tear up any treaty between
    states of mind and shut
        to the eye any vision
that does not excitedly see the infinite.

In the Desert

When grandma took me to Quetta
the train cut through sugarcane
and maize fields across the Punjab
and entered the Thar desert.

I stood at the window for hours
and watched the sand of the desert
meet the sandy beach of the sky
where the heat-haze broke in waves.

It was the first time that I'd seen
a world in which there seemed
nothing to live for and nothing
with which to keep one alive.

I had a fantasy as children do
of being alone in the desert
and lasting there for no longer
than a drop of water.

I stood at the window for hours
and wanted to know for how long
the world as far as I could see
would continue completely empty.

Now thirty years later when I look back
on that journey through the desert
I feel I am still at the window
searching the horizon for plants.

Islanders

Like water-buffalo worrying the mud-bank
of a river where the tongue can't reach
deep enough into the veins of the cracked

earth for water; or in the monsoon
months when the land sinks –
such alternatives! As with those other

islanders, cultivating the slopes
of volcanic hills, on the lip of fire,
the murderous vicinity of violence:

so on the edge of this ocean whose seas
whip our chained islands: we live
where we're most vulnerable to death.

Old Ragged Claws

What land is this from where two poets exiled
themselves? Barbarism knocks its bull's head
and sends the continents drifting, and not here
only is the beast burdensome. What land is this?

Once I used to travel with no expectation
than surprise, wanting only rivers to be wide
and plains to spread their vineyards and corn
with a deep green and for the sky to be

on its best blue behaviour. Now I read cautionary
guides and consult a travel agency about
the quality of the bathrooms before going.
Age makes cowards of us as youth makes fools.

I should have sat behind a yoke binding the bullocks
to the earth and let the sun bully my head
into submission: scratching the hard, neutral soil,
bound by horizons which the tropical haze held

in its sweaty palm. I feel still my arm-pits weep,
and dust afflict my larynx like a drought.
My voice still creaks like a bullock-cart
pursuing its wobbly ruts, and my eyes are shot

with the blood of sunsets that brought no rest.
Gone that land, slipped away with the earth's kicking
its heels, its trees uprooted for the desert's
pleasure, for the desert's thirst its rivers emptied.

Under this wintry sun trapped among wanton clouds,
at this junction of migratory routes where I
watch birds fill up a tree for an hour and then leave
it empty as a football stadium, what land is this

where fields are banked with rusting refrigerators
and beautification programmes, bringing cosmetics
to geography, fill up the earth's wrinkles with lakes?
I have come so far West, the East is near.

A Private Lot

The old wagon-train trail is still
marked in the valley, a stony,
axle-creaking track in the pine
forest, so lumped with limestone that
one imagines the wheels wobble;

the trail ends against massed boulders
while a mile away is the clear
alternative of a river
and a plain with a horizon
not bounded by a horseshoe hill

steeply banked with stunted pines.
To come here is to reach nowhere;
yet the track suggests the trail
was well used, not mistakenly
followed once by people who lost

their way. The realtor narrates
this bit of Texan lore and starts
to persuade me that I should build
in the privacy of these pines
a home I would not want to leave.

Don't Forget the Pill, Dear

Blessed are the savage lands of this world,
the hot centres, the direct links with
the sun, or the steely icicled North,
its bared wolves' teeth at one's heart;

for observe in temperate climates, in Kew,
say, the museum-clutter of trees and the ducks
splashing in the decorative lakes: ah,
the turnstile's threepenny bit of nature!

So, we assume love's strained capacities,
maintaining the gutter's respect for the street.
The sand, the snow – such extremities of
abstract assertion while here we're surrounded

by polystyrene insulated walls and the *objets
d'art* picked up in a foreign market or on some beach;
we make spring-mattressed love with its
Kleenex anti-climax, hearing the planes descend.

Sometimes I say: *To hell with it!* For
what better declaration than to applaud
when you dance like a blizzard or become
the essence of humidity in a rain-forest?

A falsification, a trick of the cultivated mind!
A *nouvelle vague* posturing or a drugstore paperback
romance I at other times think is all
that's left. The city soot which dissipates

the sun, and the fumes from the gas boiler
commit us to degeneration. Gentle cowards,
our emotions muddied with restraint, we submit
to history's fashionable misconceptions.

A Woman's Illness

Now in mid-June she can lie
beside the apple-tree believing that
the sun restores what the antibiotics,
exploding in her blood all winter, took
from her flesh, pounds of it,
her body a hostage to recovery.

Once in November she cried
the pain out, holding my hand. I was straw
to her near-drowning. I was an oxygen mask
she needed at the peak of pain. Her breath
broke down, her face crumpled
like metal on collision.

This was the winter of
miraculous surgery. She heard about it,
a cripple reading about the Olympic Games.
Of course in her own heart she knew what
she needed most: a more demonstratively
loving son than I had been.

Disfiguration

The waters of your body are murky.
You bite at the air as if it hung there
like fruit. I look at the chart, the jerky
op-art line of fluctuating temperature.

You say: water hurts your teeth when you drink.
A bite of food blows you up like a balloon.
You're draining away on the bed's white enamel sink.
I give you sips of water with a spoon.

I look round the ward with half-shut eyes. Beds
seem to be hanging from the walls, coloured
by abstract faces: pale pinks, violent reds.
And when I look at you, it is as I feared:

you are a collage of what you were, torn
with pain. You are a doodle, a pretty
picture disfigured. True likeness has gone
from the canvas of your identity.

The Geranium Man

Observe, from his trunk upwards,
his shirt blossom out wild as spring;
hear the insensible words,
the nasal voice with which he sings:
the world's lover, see him bow
to strangers (God, anything
and nothing are significant!),
this admirable innocent,
holy as a Hindu cow.

The budgerigar bells, the long
hair, this geranium man in his pot,
what he sings is not a song
and what he thinks is not a thought.
Blown-up poster gestures for speech
(O but his metaphysics cannot
bear words), he applauds purities
whose own ecstasy lies
in the real being out of reach.

The Ant and the Mosquito

Followers of strict codes, policed
into one-way systems, the ants
carry on their business with the least
fuss: killers, devourers of plants,
but efficient, quiet.

Urbane, civil, never a beast,
now one may stray into a bowl
of sugar, now another feast
upon a fallen fig: but ants all
are virtuously silent.

Not the mosquito, that unique
pest: kill one between clapping hands,
another comes: physically weak,
of little substance, it demands
attention, response.

It will enter the ear to speak
what one has heard it say before:
not straightforward, plain, but oblique,
devious its menace: an utter bore,
its product a disease.

ZULFIKAR GHOSE

The Remove

The Sikh from Ambala in East Punjab,
India, formerly in the British Empire,
the Muslim from Sialkot in West Punjab,
Pakistan, formerly British India,
the Sikh boy and the Muslim boy are two
of twenty such Sikhs and Muslims
from East Punjab and West Punjab, which
formerly were the Punjab,
standing together in assembly, fearfully
miming the words of a Christian hymn.

Later, their firework voices explode
in Punjabi until Mr Iqbal –
which can be a Sikh name or a Muslim name,
Mohammed Iqbal or Iqbal *Singh* –
who comes from Jullundur in East Punjab
but near enough to the border to be almost
West Punjab, who is a specialist in
the archaic intonations of the *Raj*,
until the three-piece-suited Mr Iqbal
gives a stiff-collared voice to his
Punjabi command to shut their thick wet
lips on the scattering sparks of their
white Secondary Modern teeth.

Mr Iqbal has come to London to teach
English to Punjabi Sikhs and Muslims
and has pinned up in his class pictures
of Gandhi and Jinnah, Nehru and Ayub
in case the parents come to ask in Punjabi
how the kids are doing in English.

And so: twenty years after
the Union Jack came down on Delhi
and the Punjab became East Punjab and
West Punjab and the Sikhs did not like it
and the Muslims did not like the Sikhs
not liking it and they killed each other
not by the hundred nor by the thousand
but by the hundred thousand, here then
is Mr Iqbal with his remove class of
twenty Punjabis, some Sikh and some Muslim,
in a Secondary Modern School in London,
all of them trying to learn English.

Back home the fastidious guardians of freedom,
the Sikh army and the Muslim army, convinced
that East is East and West is West etcetera,
periodically accuse each other of aggression.

B. S. JOHNSON

Living By

Walking, snow falling, it is possible
to focus at various distances
in turn on separate flakes, sharply engage
the attention at several spatial points:
the nearer cold and more uncomfortable,
the farther distanced and almost pleasing.

Living, time passing, it is preferable
to focus the memory in turn upon
the more distant retrospects in order
that the present mind may retain its peace.

Yet knowing that seeing and remembering
are both of course personal illusions.

Evening: Barents Sea

the trawl of unquiet mind drops astern

great lucid streamers bar the sky ahead
(bifurcated banners at a tourney)
light alchemizes the brass on the bridge
into sallow gold
                    now the short northern
autumn day closes quickly

                        the thin coast
(of grey Norway is it, or of Russia?)
distinguished only as a formal change
in the pattern of clouds on our port side

on deck the strung lights illuminate no
movement but the sullen swill of water
in the washer, but the unnatural way
dead starfish and disregarded dabs swim
in the strict seas surging through the bilges
and out. A fishgut hangs like a hank of
hair from the iron grill in a pound board

brighter now than the sun, the fishfinder's
green bleep catches the skipper's intentness

and the trawl is down, is out, is catching!

Brought Very Close

Brought very close to death by one world war,
my grandfather chose to die just in time
to avoid being killed by the next one.
My grandmother, wise after the bombing
and seeing benefit in everything,
said, *Just as well, for he'd not have stood it*.
She did, and showed everyone the neat hole
burned through the old table in the outside
back area by a hissing whitehot
incendiary bomb, but told no one except
my father how she calmly saved her home.
In the same night the proud church opposite
became a gutted smoking shell of stone:
her old eyes laughed as she drew the moral.

At Eight Years Old

At eight years old one summer afternoon
they took me to the Victoria Palace to see
Lupino Lane, when I would just as soon
have stayed at home in the Hammersmith garden, free.
Afterwards, they made for a nearby pub,
and as they went I heard them speak of war;
I fidgeted; my pants began to rub;
I belched my lemonade outside the door.
Inside they met Lupino Lane, and brought
him out for me; his front teeth were decayed;
I forget now what he said, although I thought
it worth remembering at the time, but paid
him shy-eyed homage as I felt I ought:
for this he bought me another lemonade.

B. S. JOHNSON

Love – All

The decorously informative church
Guide to Sex suggested that any urge
could well be controlled by playing tennis:
and the game provided also 'many
harmless opportunities for healthy
social intercourse between the sexes'.

For weeks the drawings in the *Guide* misled
me as to what went where, but nonetheless
I booked the public courts and learnt the game
with other curious youths of my age:
and later joined a club, to lose six one,
six love, in the first round of the Open.

But the only girl I ever met had
her 'energies channelled' far too bloody
'healthily', and very quickly let me
know that love was merely another means
of saying nil. It was not as though I
became any good at tennis, either.

Daughter

One early potential father-in-law of mine
sang sad songs when he was drunk, tearfully,
spoke of me man to man over port-style wine,
and urged his daughter not to marry me.

Her mother savaged carpets on a line,
all Catholic Irishness, and cheerfully
suffered to have me visit once to dine,
but urged her daughter not to marry me.

This girl took more in love from me than nine
other, later, loves: observing fearfully,
I wondered why her parents should combine
to urge their daughter not to marry me.

Then, seeing further than I wished to see,
I urged their daughter not to marry me.

B. S. JOHNSON

Great Man

What was it like to
live then? we asked him,
who had lived through it.

Bad, he said, it was
not good. I envy
you missing it all.

He seemed bored by our
questions, interested
more in our women.

A Dublin Unicorn

'... *his virtue is no less famous than his strength, in that his horn is supposed to be the most powerful antidote against poison: inasmuch as the general conceit is, that the wild beasts of the wilderness use not to drink of the pools, for fear of the venomous serpents there breeding, before the unicorn hath stirred it with his horn ... and by the keen scent he hath, he can detect a maiden afar off and will run to her, and lay down his head in her lap ...*'

I

Not by nature simple, as his end might
possibly suggest, the unicorn to
a large extent enjoyed his vocation:
such he called it, this holy business of

purifying the means of life for those
unable to perform it for themselves;
but otherwise he kept for the most part
to the desert, and lived solitary

near the tops of high mountains, feeding as
he found, and going as he liked; content
in knowledge that his life was not without
some use, and pleased to live the life he wished.

No thought of harm occurred to him that day
in the heavy forest when he saw the
virgin; homage came as naturally to
him as cleansing to the deep pools he stirred.

And it was natural, too, to lay his head
in the soft lap of this young virgin, and

look upward to her face in trust and peace:
and then the arrow juddered in his flank.

In that short pause between his dying and
his death, the unicorn made some attempt
to understand the virgin's betrayal:
but died, seeing her tears, still more confused.

2

When he asked her, it seemed so exciting:
a proof, too, of her purity: for though
they said virginity was more a state
of mind than physical intactness, it

could yet do a girl no harm to have some
positive proof; and especially since the
usual tests seemed to end in the loss of
that which they were calculated to prove.

Exciting, too, rising in the early
morning, and hearing the dogs barking near
the stables, and swaying through the heavy
forest on her mare, behind the hunter;

and even when she was sitting on the
grass, toying with leaves, and the hunter had
withdrawn, she was excited at thoughts of
the kill: but then she saw the unicorn.

Proudly and humbly it laid its silver
head and golden horn down in her lap, and
looked upward to her face in trust and peace:
and then the arrow juddered in its flank.

Her horror made her wish the arrow had
struck her instead, but it was unicorn's
blood upon her thighs; her tears were too late
now, and virginity was meaningless.

3

To the hunter, it was really just a
job: the church had ordered the destruction
of all mythical, unchristian creatures,
and doubtless those who gave the order knew

exactly what they were about. He was
engaged, he told himself whenever the
slaughter disturbed his simple peace, not to
question orders but to execute them.

And he took a certain pride in his work;
there were not many knew as well as he
the ways of unicorns and other beasts,
and none so consistent in their killing.

Now, in the heavy forest, he placed the
virgin where she might be clearly seen, and
where he judged the unicorn would seek her;
the hunter then withdrew, flighting a shaft.

Just as he had hoped, the unicorn laid
down its head in the virgin's soft lap, and
looked upwards to her face in trust and peace:
and then his arrow juddered in its flank.

Another unicorn! the hunter said,
Why do I never catch the rarer beasts?
Only the creatures of the forest mourned,
and the virgin, whose tears were too late now.

In Yates's

So: there's this bird with the orange
   hair who played piano of a kind
while a unicephaloid
   accompanied not far behind.

I'll be loving you. Always,
   he sang. One love swore. Though the cow
at least had guilt enough to be
   sorry her always didn't mean now.

A Russian seaman then divulged
   that there were bad English and good
Russians, oh, and insisted further:
   I haf fife times lost my blood!

Smoke incensed the wineheavy air:
   two lovers made a winelodge vow:
and I have five times lost my blood
   because always didn't mean now.

Bad News for Her Mother

Yes, I shall write it all down, you old cow,
all: the first time, the last time, all the times
in between, and then all the times I should
have liked there to have been. I shall go on
writing it down even out of habit,
till there is nothing left to exorcise.

You may judge from that the emotional
debt I feel your lovely daughter owes me.

B. S. JOHNSON

Spatial Definition

Razed the room in which
we made so much love:

I try to re-place
it in space against
the windracked planetrees:

my eyes quarter air.

Theatregoer

Somewhere some nights she sees
curtains rise on those rites
we also knew and felt

I sit here desolate
in spite of company

Love is between people

Driving

Concentration may be less than total:

the disposition of crockets on a
Gothic finial, a fat woman's gait,
the way quartz intrusions scar a mountain's
jowl, and speculation on the local
incidence of – say – foot and mouth disease:

all these are safely objects of remark,
others and all these may well engage a
safe proportion of my mind when driving:

but how dangerous then to think of her!

Too Many Flesh Suppers

Abstracted in art,
in architecture,
in scholars' detail;

absorbed by music,
by minutiae,
by sad trivia;

all to efface her,
whom I can forget
no more than breathing.

B. S. JOHNSON

And Should She Die?

And should she die tonight,
with this three years' difference
as well between us now?

Or no, be maimed perhaps
and bearing pain, to live
on damages for life?

In any case, I wish
her no good, whom I loved
as Brunel loved iron.

Myddelton Square

They gave proportion to this Square by walls
patterned with glass, due space between each stack,
lined stucco fronts, and subtly pitched roof-falls:
yet, one side, left a gap a house-width wide
through which one has a Prospect of St Paul's.

This I resemble, in that, till you died
my life was ordered but now has a lack
through which I have a prospect that appals.

Restoration

Wren defined the London air with spires,
restored a city gored by mindless fires:

so I on ruins try to build the new,
define the void left thoughtlessly by you.

Image in Provence

Her face suddenly, on this mountain road:
(cypresses guttering like black candleflames
there in the valley, still hawk over high
eroded limestone left, right lavender
clumps close-shorn to purple-stubbled naevi):
that face suddenly, the shape exactly,
the lost eyes spanning a cleft in the cloud
smiling in the first way I remember:
the known against this visited landscape.

I had ceased to think of her as having
this face, any face: she was an idea,
an area of pain, a wound, a death.

The hawk of the past stooped, ripped at my mind,
left me with an equivocal freedom.

Arrived at the Place

Arrived at the place
to which I always
said I was going:

comfortless for lack
of her who chose not
to travel with me:

too aware my way
to wherever next
is also alone.

Knowing

Knowledge of her was
earned like miners' pay:

afterwards I sought
friends' knowledge of her:

now I need to know
nothing of this girl:

she whom I once knew
as my tongue my mouth:

Good News for Her Mother!

Probably the Last Poem I Shall Write About Her Daughter

In the last year ending with eight (cunningly
making it timeless) ten years ago, that is,
I was in this pub with this girl, or that girl,
whichever, the one girl, anyway, one one:
and it was very clear, then, at that time, here
that she didn't reckon I'd ever make it
(not sexually, you misunderstand me, yes,
that was soon settled, and fair it was, too. Ah.)

Where was I? In this pub, where I am now, yes,
with this girl I was with (in most senses) then,
and she was convinced I would never get there,
wherever it was she wanted me to get.

I sat swollen, drowned in her cruel certainty.

It was all tied up with supremacy, power,
for she could never beat me at anything
(except being a woman, at which I have
never, even in the prenatal stages
of bisexuality, been very good);
and so she used the only weapon she had,
which was unexpectedly to betray me
at Xmas, which has always been a bad time
for me ever since they first told me that there
was not, and never had been, a Santa Claus.

But here I am then, still, fatter and having
got more or less where I said I was going,

in the theatre pub where then even to have
spoken to one of the actors would have been
as hard as writing a play is now. I stand
arguing with the artistic director
(who I now think an untalented cretin)
full of contempt for the lack of serious
intent in what he conceives to be drama.

And what strikes me now is not that she was wrong
(which *Heaven forfend!* as they say) but that it
would not matter even if she had been right.

B. S. JOHNSON

Porth Ceiriad Bay

Descended to the shore, odd how we left
the young girl with us to herself, and went
straight to examine the stratified cliffs,
forgot her entirely in our interest.

You marvelled at the shapes the clockwork sea
had worn the stone, talking keenly, until
the pace of this random sculpture recalled
your age to you, and then its anodynes.

And so you turned, pretending youth, courting
the girl as if you were a boy again,
leaving the wry cliffs to their erosion
and me to my observant solitude.

from the sequence *Cwm Pennant*

3

This lean fivefloored tower was built
to give a father's sons
scholarly solitude and peace,
a study-floor to each;

but trees had long ago engaged
the tower's lichened height,
and were within a year or two
of hiding every sign

of its existence on the hill,
but for the gaunt flagstaff;
outwardly the fabric was sound,
founded upon outcropped

slate in which pyrites glinted
against rusty oxide:
inside, however, looking up,
the few joists were patterned

against the summer like broken
teeth in an unwashed comb,
and the doorless and windeyeless
weeping walls stared glibly.

Stone treads wound safe and square inside
the shell towards the lip,
past architraves embossed with each
son's Oxford college arms;

heraldic beasts with weather-smudged
features maintained shy guard
on leaden remnants of a roof;
stones fell within a flue,

making the dry silence; a post
office van scuttered down
this valley of Cwm Pennant like
a spotless ladybird.

The top stair offered abeyance;
at my feet a spider
ran across his dusty network
to paralyse a bee;

I freed the captive with a twig,
and the spider retired:
two disrupters of his peace who
bore him no benefit.

His disappointment, the tower's
desolation, and my
chosen solitude, aloofness,
correlated within

my mind, and I stilled at the thought
that disappointment might
transmute solitude to glib and
eyeless desolation.

5

Salmon are fairly easy fish to gaff,
provided you have once located them;
and the sporting men who call such methods
foul conveniently ignore in their
  own fishing the element of deceit:
  concealing hooks in something meant to eat.

But arguments like this would hardly help
dissuade the water bailiff if he caught
you, so you palm the two-inch hook until
the last moment (that, meeting him by chance,
  you could then quietly drop it when you wish)
  and cut a stick when you have found a fish.

You see a place where flowing tails have fanned
the gravel clean, and know that underneath
the bank just there the fasting salmon lie.
The handforged hook you socket to the stick
  and wind its cord quite loosely up its length,
  but, striking, grasp the end with all your strength.

David and I would hold each other safe
by turns while one hung down the rootboned bank,
his hair streaming in the Dwyfor's current,
and move the gaff (oh slowly, slowly!) down
  and beneath the salmon's gunmetal flank
  till nothing of it could be seen but shank.

Since I could never judge sufficiently
the gaff's refraction in the running stream,
I hooked no salmon; but when David did
my part was then to leave the bank with it,
  slewing and bucking against the barb's bite,
  and run as far and quickly as I might.

Then he would follow, seize and stun the fish,
and, one grey eye out for the bailiff, bring
it to the high-roomed granite farmhouse where
his parents and his sister, he and I,
    would celebrate this ending to a life:
    the salmon I had sought still suffered life.

In the Ember Days of My Last Free Summer

In the ember days of my last free summer,
here I lie, outside myself, watching
the gross body eating a poor curry:
satisfied at what I have done, scared of what
I have to do in my last free winter.

The Bonepit Testes Series

On the third day we came to the bonepit
People it seemed had been there before us
It was distressing that they had not left
The bones as they would have wished to find them

We had first to clear a space for our match
Then we set up fibulae for wickets
The longer phalanges made ducky bails
While for bats and ball we used male femurs
And a whole green fossilized testicle

It is they say important to keep fit

The Dishonesty of Metaphor

The sound of rain
is like only
the sound of rain

(rain seen against
the black threat of
copper beeches)

in truth can be
like nothing but
the sound of rain

Preconception

I have no children:

but tonight a poem came
in which a small child,
my daughter, appeared at the door
of a half-lit room
where late one night I wrote
at a heavy desk.

And though interruption
was hardly welcome
I took her to myself,
just as the poem,
comforted this daughter
until she found peace.

The poems as the children
come as they will come.

Change is the Only Constant

Unpleasurably I remark the coming
of the winter of my last childless year:
pawnbroker seeds, skeletal bankrupt leaves
still adhere, it does not seem desperately,
certainly it does not seem joyfully,
into December of this barren year.
One leaf for the third day flaps like a bird,
a pigeon held in a high wind feathers
for an instant like a fat urban hawk,
and client gulls pose coldly on the long
dormer opposite: I shall not feed them
this or any other brackish morning,
I who have welcomed winter (as any
season) must see the child is welcome now.

B. S. JOHNSON

Occupation: Father

My son finds occupation
in almost nothing, in everything:
my soapy penitential toothpaste,
his mother's loosened hair,
orts, containers, useless things;
watches as I pee
as at Victoria Falls,
once pushed his head between my knees
to risk some sort of baptism.

Before his birth I thought
I had room for no more love:
now when he (say) hurts himself
love, consideration, care
(copies from the originals)
as if burst inside me.

Undoggedly I interest myself
in his uninteresting concerns,
grow backward to him,
more than hoping to find
a forward interest for myself.

The Poet Holds His Future in His Hand

Tonight I looked at it: I don't often

it performs its two functions well enough
in return I keep it reasonably clean

but quite by chance I looked at it tonight
and there were several dirty marks on it

I of course looked harder: and they were veins
underneath the skin, bloody great black veins!

they weren't there last time I happened to look
certainly the light was bad in that place

but there's no doubt that the pressure is on

B. S. JOHNSON

Chart Me

To His Wife

Chart me as I grow

middleaging hands
which are mine

you are five
years younger

Chart me as I go

No, I've Not

Those breasts you
loved to weigh
by handsful,
dint, pucker,
have fallen
now: I think
– with something
like the old
vanity –
as far as
they will fall.

Those nipples
which once stood
pleasured to
the lightest
running of
your fingers
are gross, brown
brindled now,
unsightly.

Those other
labia
your wet tongue
at first so
shockingly
found, researched,
are dry now,
admit to
emptiness,
a disused
worked-out mine.

Their answer:
No, I've not
remarried.

Where Is the Sprinkler Stop Valve?

Urinating in a urinal
I try at first directly
to jet down a fruitfly
then see random sprinkling
is the proper method –

you cannot beat the random element

as in cancer, as my mother knew

B. S. JOHNSON

Food for Cancerous Thought

The small betrayals
eat us all away

the work done for less
than the minimum

the lickerish glance
at another girl

the long snack taken
just before a meal

But we shall
be eaten away
anyway

The Short Fear

My awkward grossness grows: I go down, through

I maintain my self in the conviction
that I have as much to say as others
and more apposite ways of saying it

Certainly I feel it has all been said

The short fear is that even saying it
in my own way is equally pointless

B. S. JOHNSON

Distance Piece

I may reach a point
   one reaches a point
where all I might have to say
   where all that one has to say
would be that life is bloody awful
   is that the human condition is intolerable
but that I would not end it
   but one resolves to go on
despite everything
   despite everything